T0208299

THE GOSHEN DILEMMA

THE GOSHEN DILEMMA

Stuart E. Heflin Sr.

authorHOUSE®

AuthorHouse™
1663 Liberty Drive
Bloomington, IN 47403
www.authorhouse.com
Phone: 1-800-839-8640

First published by AuthorHouse   07/13/2011

ISBN: 978-1-4567-6609-2 (sc)
ISBN: 978-1-4567-6640-5 (ebk)

Library of Congress Control Number: 2011907434

Printed in the United States of America

Any people depicted in stock imagery provided by Thinkstock are models, and such images are being used for illustrative purposes only.
Certain stock imagery © Thinkstock.

This book is printed on acid-free paper.

I dedicate this book to
Stuart Jr., Ryan, Angelo,
Galen and Quincy Heflin,
with special gratitude to Galen,
Quincy and my wife, Sheila,
for their special support on this project.

My ultimate wishes are that my five
golden sons continue their successful
patterns, and that they would eliminate
any formidable dross that may be festering in their
precious hearts and lives and grow to be the spiritual
warriors God designed them to be.

Special love to my mother, Mary
and my sisters, Cheryl, Joyce and Debbie.

Prelude

SCRIPTURE SAYS THAT there is nothing new under the sun, and what has been will be again (Ecclesiastes 1:9 KJV). This scripture is the pivot for the analogies of this book. I will couple many past events and parallel them with twentieth and twenty-first century events in America. This will require a modicum of imagination, and sometimes pure faith. I implore you to not simply read this book, but examine it thoroughly with the Word. I will justify claims in this book strictly using documented research and the Word, so feel free to draw your own conclusions. My primary intention is not to inflict pain, derail beliefs or ignite malice or fear in any individual or group. Good pastors, beloved by your congregations, keep inspiring God's flock and be not offended by any part of this book. Take a journey with me back through time. Although some analogies may be painful, stay with me until the end, and you will see the light of the Goshen Dilemma.

Chapter 1

Mizraim-Egypt

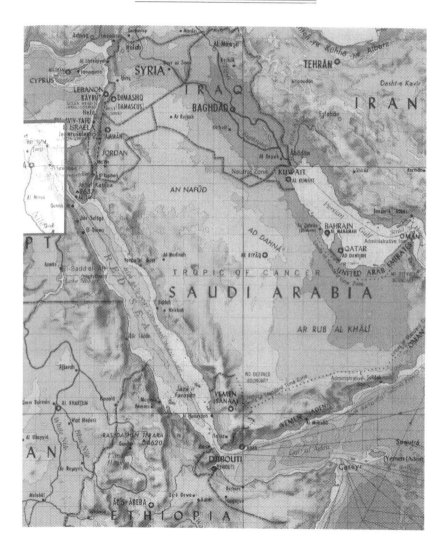

JACOB, THE FATHER OF MANY SONS, fathered one son who would become the savior of a powerful nation. The son, Joseph, was sold into slavery by his brothers, to merchants as they journeyed to the ancient metropolis of Egypt. His brothers despised him because of his prophetic dreams and heavenly visions that depicted him as a great dignitary, one to whom they all would pay homage. He also was one of the youngest of Jacob's children, born of Jacob's beloved Rachel in Jacob's later years. Even as God allowed misfortune to befall him, Joseph was a man of integrity, and he was chosen by God for a special purpose.

Because of his God given supernatural wisdom, Joseph was able to interpret dreams. Imprisoned for an alleged sexual impropriety with Pharaoh's captain of the guard's wife, his gift of dream interpretation elevated him from the prison into the presence of Pharaoh. Pharaoh, ruler of Egypt, whose deities included bovine animals such as Apis and Hathor, was given dreams that involved fat and lean cows. No one in Egypt could interpret these troublesome dreams. Joseph interpreted Pharaoh's dreams, which prevented Egypt from being consumed by seven years of famine. Joseph's precise interpretation of the dreams landed him in the high cabinet of the pharaoh. Joseph became second in command of great Egypt under the great Pharaoh. (Genesis 41:38-45)

Egypt was one of the earliest and most powerful civilizations of this world. It is situated on the Nile River in northeastern Africa. Even today, there are many magnificent historical wonders there for all mankind to see and ponder. Goshen (Rameses) was one of the most fertile regions of Egypt, in a region were there are many river deltas. It was considered the best area in Egypt in ancient times (Genesis 45:18-20). Goshen was the region that Pharaoh gave to Joseph's people to inhabit once Joseph had risen to be the vice president of Egypt.

Just as Goshen was the choicest section of Egypt, many cities of America have sections that have historically been considered the most desirable locations to live in. For decades some of these areas were "Red Lined" to prevent subcultures from inhabiting them. In the city where I reside, I remember how beautiful the lower Dayton View area was in the sixties. It was a pristine place with white picket fences and cultivated lawns. It was undeniably a "Leave it to Beaver" neighborhood.

> **Pharaoh** [PHAY row]—the title of the kings of Egypt until 323 BC, meaning "Great House", originally referred to the king's palace, but by the reign of Thutmose III (1479-1425 BC) in the New Kingdom had become a form of address for the person of the king. The Egyptian term for the ruler himself was *nsw(t)-bjt(j)* (rendered in Babylonian as *insibya*; Egyptological pronunciation "*Nesu(t)-Bit(i)*"), "King of Upper and Lower Egypt", literally "he of the sedge and the bee" (properly nj-sw.t-bj.t), the sedge and the bee being the symbols for Upper and Lower Egypt, respectively. Also *nsw.t-t3wj* "King of the Two Lands". This double kingship was expressed in the *Pschent*, the double crown combining the red crown of Lower Egypt (*Deshret*) and the white crown of Upper Egypt (*Hedjet*).

Initially the rulers were considered the sons of the cow deity Bat and later Hathor, whose throne they occupied to rule the country and officiate in religious rituals. There is evidence that the ruler may have been sacrificed in the earliest rituals, but soon these rituals replaced the ruler with a specially selected bull. Late in the culture the pharaohs were believed to be the incarnations of the deity Horus in life and Osiris in death. Once the cult of Isis and Osiris became prominent, pharaohs were viewed as a bridge between the god Osiris and human beings; and after death the pharaoh was believed to unite with Osiris. The royal line was matriarchal and a relationship with the royal women through birth or marriage (or both) determined the right to rule. The royal women played important roles in the religious rituals and governance of the country, sometimes participating alongside the pharaoh.

Pharaoh from Wikipedia, the free encyclopedia

Many powerful kings who ruled Egypt were called by different titles according to their dynasties. For instance, the name of the king in Egypt during the time of Moses was Pharaoh Rameses II. When the pharaoh died, Egyptians believed that he became the god Osiris, the ruler of the underworld and those who live after death. The pharaoh was the head of the army as well as a central figure in the nation's religious life. As an intermediate between gods and people, the pharaoh functioned as a high priest in the many temples in Egypt

Chapter 2

PHARAOH'S DILEMMA

AFTER MANY YEARS, The Hebrew immigrant population grew in Goshen. Pharaoh perceived this as a monumental problem. He became concerned about the allegiance of all the Hebrew immigrants living within his borders (Exodus 1:7-10), fearing that they might fight on the side of Pharaoh's enemies, or cause a coup and effect regime change. Pharaoh and his cabinet officers decided to use subterfuge for control, and he began to enslave the Hebrew people. The Egyptians no longer remembered Joseph and how that he had delivered the kingdom some 400 years prior in a time of severe famine (Genesis 41:35-). Pharaoh subjected the Hebrews to build Pithom and Rameses his great storehouse cities. Pharaoh directed his governors to make the people serve with rigor. This is the genesis of the modern phrase "working me like a Hebrew slave".

Slave Master Willie Lynch's instructions to slave owners at a 1712 conference on the banks of the James River in Jamestown, Virginia are widely known. He instructed the slavers how they should handle slaves in the new America. His keynote address reads thus:

> Gentlemen:
> I greet you here on the bank of the James River in the year of our lord, one thousand seven hundred and twelve. First, I shall thank you, the gentlemen of the colony of Virginia, for bringing me here. I am here to help you solve some of your problems with slaves. Your invitation reached me in my modest plantation in the West Indies where I have experimented with some of the newest and still the oldest method for control of slaves. Ancient Rome would envy us if my program were implemented. As our boat sailed south on the James River, named for our illustrious King James, whose Bible we cherish, I saw enough to know that our problem is not unique. While Rome used cords or wood as crosses for standing human bodies along the old highways in great numbers, you are here using the tree and the rope on occasion.

I caught the whiff of a dead slave hanging from a tree a couple of miles back. You are losing valuable stock by hangings, you are having uprisings, slaves are running away, your crops are sometimes left in the fields too long for maximum profit, you suffer occasional fires, your animals are killed, Gentleman, You know what your problems are; I do not need to elaborate. I am not here to enumerate your problems; I am here to introduce you to a method of solving them.

In my bag, I have a foolproof method for controlling your slaves. I guarantee every one of you that if installed it will control the slaves for at least three hundred years. My method is simple, any member of your family or any overseer can use it.

I have outlined a number of differences among the slaves, and I take these differences and make them bigger. I use **Fear, Distrust, and Envy** for control purposes. These methods have worked on my modest plantation in the West Indies, and it will work throughout the South. Take this simple little list of differences and think about them. On the top of my list is "**Age**" but it is only there because it starts with an "A"; The second is "**Color**" or shade; there is **Intelligence, Size, Sex, Size of plantation, Attitude of owner**, whether the slaves live in the valley, on a hill, east or west, north, south, have fine or coarse hair, or is tall or short. Now that you have a list of differences, I shall give you an outline of action—but before that, I shall assure you that DISTRUST IS STRONGER THAN TRUST, AND ENVY IS STRONGER THAN ADULATION, RESPECT OR ADMIRATION. The black slave, after receiving this indoctrination, shall carry on and will become self-refueling and self-generating for hundreds of years, maybe thousands.

Don't forget you must pitch the old black VS. the young black males, and the young black male against the old black male. You must use the dark skinned slaves VS. the light skin slaves. You must use the female VS the male, and the male VS, the female. You must always have your servants and OVERSEERS distrust all blacks, but it is necessary that your slaves trust and depend on us. Gentlemen, these kits are your keys to control, use them. Never miss an opportunity. My plan is guaranteed, and the good thing about this plan is that if used intensely for one year the slave will remain perpetually distrustful.
-WILLIAM LYNCH-1712 (*Willie Lynch from thetalkingdrum.com*)

Just as the Egyptian no longer remembered Joseph, likewise the African Americans do not exist in history. Although the African Americans are responsible for much of modern life, the history of the African American has been deliberately omitted from most modern textbooks.

With all the immigrants in America today and with the threat of modern terrorism, the issue of racial profiling continues to resurface. The Black community has coined phrases like "driving while black", or "standing while black", meaning that you could be apprehended by law enforcement officers for no other crime than just doing anything and being African American. Those of Hispanic descent or Middle Eastern descent and some economically challenged Caucasians have similar experiences. The Tea Party movement continually expresses concerns similar to Pharaoh's with statements like, "If we don't do something right now, we will lose our country; we are taking it back from all these liberals and socialists."

Chapter 3

DIRTY MIDWIVES

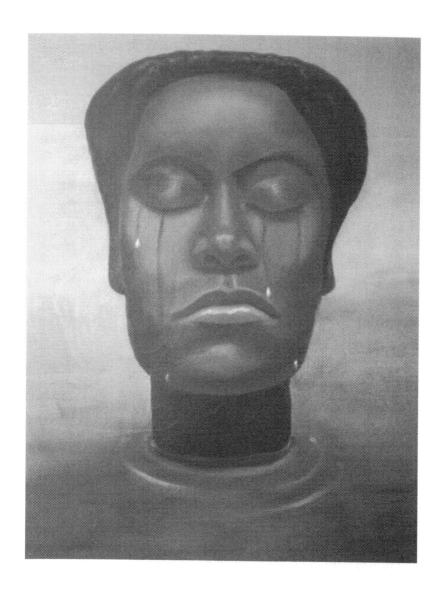

CONTINUING HIS NEED FOR CONTROL, Pharaoh proclaimed an edict. He ordered the Hebrew midwives to kill Hebrew children. His primary focus was to annihilate Hebrew males and control the Hebrew population through genocide (Exodus 1:15-22). When the Hebrew midwives did not comply out of fear of God, Pharaoh ordered everyone to cast all the baby Hebrew males into the Nile River. He wanted the Hebrew women to kill their own male babies. Many babies were drowned in the Nile River, and this circumstance created dirty midwives.

In 1973 the U.S. Supreme Court ruled in its Roe v. Wade decision that unborn babies were not legal "persons". From that point on they have no rights or protection under our constitution. Since that time, over 45,000,000 babies have been put to death by abortion in this country according to Heritage House Literature. Author and feminist leader Gloria Steinman was quoted on CNN, September 9, 1981, "A woman would have the right to abortion just as she has the right to remove any parasitic growth from her body." In 1980, Dr. Martii Kekomaki justified conduction experiments involving slicing open the stomachs and cutting off the heads of live late term aborted babies, "An aborted baby is just garbage and that's where it ends up," he declared, "Why not make use of it for society?" (National Examiner 8-19-1980)

How Are Abortions Performed?

1. In the Suction Aspiration method, the cervical muscle ring must be paralyzed and stretched open. The abortionist then inserts a hollow plastic tube with a knife-like edge into the uterus. The suction tears the baby's body into pieces. The placenta is cut from the uterine wall and everything is sucked into a bottle.

2. RU-486 abortions are done after a mother misses her period. It can be used up to the second month of pregnancy. It works by blocking

progesterone, a crucial hormone during pregnancy. Without it, the uterine lining does not provide food, fluid and oxygen to the tiny developing baby. The baby can not survive. A second drug is then given that stimulates the uterus to contract and the baby is expelled.

3. Prostaglandin is a hormone that induces abortion in mid to late term pregnancies. The baby usually dies from the trauma of the delivery. However, if the baby is old enough, it is born alive. This is called a "complication." To prevent this some abortionist use ultrasound to guide them as they inject a drug into the unborn baby's heart that kills the fetus. Prostaglandin is then administered and the dead baby is delivered.

4. Dilation and Curettage (D&C) is similar to a suction procedure except a curette, a loop shaped steel knife, is inserted into the uterus at 6 to 12 weeks of pregnancy. The baby and the placenta are cut into pieces and scraped out into a basin. Bleeding is usually heavy with this method.

5. Dilation and Evacuation (D&E) is done after the third month. The cervix must be dilated before the abortion. Usually Laminaria sticks are inserted into the cervix. These are made of seaweed that is compressed into thin sticks. When inserted, they absorb moisture and expand, thus enlarging the cervix. A pliers-like instrument is inserted through the cervix into the uterus. The abortionist then seizes a leg, arm or other part of the baby, and with a twisting motion, tears it from the body. This continues until only the head remains. Finally, the skull is crushed and pulled out. The nurse must reassemble the body parts to be sure all of them were removed.

6. The Partial Birth Abortion or Dilation and Extraction (D&X) abortion method is also used on mid and late term babies, from 4 to 9 months'

gestation. Ultrasound is used to identify how the baby is facing in the womb. The abortionist inserts forceps through the cervical canal into the uterus and grasps one of the baby's legs, positioning the baby feet first, face down (breech position). The child's body is then pulled out of the birth canal except for the head, which is too large to pass through the cervix. The baby is alive and probably kicking and flailing his legs and arms. The abortionist hooks his fingers over the baby's shoulder, holding the woman's cervix away from the baby's neck. He then jams blunt tipped surgical scissors into the base of the skull and spreads the tips apart to enlarge the wound. A suction catheter is inserted into the baby's skull and the brain is sucked out. The skull collapses and the baby's head passes easily through the cervix. (Heritage House Literature)

A distinction was made between the baby boys and the baby girls of Goshen. The females were allowed to survive and integrate into Egyptian society. Although exploited, this was some relief to Hebrew women and their daughters. Moses' sister, Miriam, was free to approach Pharaoh's daughter when Moses was discovered in the reeds. She solicited Pharaoh's daughter if she desired a nurse for the baby. Moses was not destroyed because his mother had a revelation that he was a goodly child (Exodus 2:2). He ultimately matured and became a prince in Egypt. I am astonished at the pseudo freedom that the Hebrew female experienced, as opposed to the perpetual doom of her male counterpart. He did not have a ghost of a chance in that great society?

Shades of Willie Lynch surfaces in modern America as African American females appear to be more integrated into American society while her male counterpart experiences the genocide of "incarceration". According to the U.S. Department of Justice, when comparing the incarceration rates to the American residential population, in 2007 black males were 6 times and Hispanic males were 2 times more likely to be held in custody than white males. Of the 2.1 million male inmates in jail or prison, black males represent the largest percentage 35.4%. (Black Demographics. com). Occasionally, a black male escapes the doldrums of prison cells or physical death on the streets, making him into a prince among his people.

Many women today abort their babies, and some are just natural born killers. Some mothers will gird up the loins of their minds and bear responsibility for their momentary passion or temporary insanity, even though it's extremely difficult. It is hard to raise children today even in a family with mom and dad present. Alone, it is virtually impossible to accomplish with all the bad influences of a morally decadent society. But every now and then a "Black Moses" emerges from the rushes. I read an article in *Jet Magazine* about entrepretainer Nick Cannon and how his mother, at age 17, ignored people who tried to coax her into having an abortion. She made the right choice and gave birth to Nick, who grew to be an assiduous, outstanding, young "Black Moses". He is largely successful, and he creates opportunities for other people to do likewise. Other black males have overcome the depravity of poverty, prison, gangs and violence prevalent in their community. "Let them live." No one knows who or what a child might become if you don't just fade them.

Pharaoh's daughter paradoxically adopted Moses, a male Hebrew child in an ominous time for all Hebrew male children. Today, wealthy white Americans adopt children of color from around the world. This is a life choice whose time has come. Good for you if your concern for mankind transcends the color line and race barriers.

Chapter 4

STAY OUT OF GOSHEN

STAY OUT OF GOSHEN. Although this command was not actually spoken by Pharaoh, it was probably a widely accepted tenet upheld by the Egyptian people. The Hebrew people, Joseph's descendants, were generally considered to be nomadic shepherds by the urban Egyptian society. Goshen was their quarantine because the Egyptians had a major disdain for the shepherd occupation (Genesis 46:34). Furthermore, the bovine animal was considered sacred (Apis bull and Hathor heifer) to the Egyptians. Pharaoh commissioned the Hebrews to manage his own animals because they were most qualified, but this wonderful area, Goshen, became a great slave pit.

In today's society, many subcultures are quarantined to certain areas of cities and are useful for menial occupations. These occupations are the sort that mainstream society finds beneficial for maintaining their own economy and lifestyle. These people are generally qualified for domestic work, harvesting, manufacturing, labor work, food and lawn services and even some commercial entertainment. As a whole, they are not a highly technically skilled people, possess minimal education, and they are not very popular or accepted outside of their quarantine. These individuals are somehow resourceful and learn to adapt to difficult situations. One Hip Hop artist said it like this, "I can not be faded, I'm a N*** from the m-f streets." Meaning, in the hood (ghetto) we keep on surviving no matter what is done to us.

Statistics show that places like East Orange, New Jersey, a city that is about 89% African American population, towers above the national average in crimes of rape, robbery, assault, burglary and auto theft. Among U.S. cities with a population of 100,000 or more, Gary, Indiana, about 84% black, experiences similar crime statistics. Gary's affluent and middle class residents relocated to surrounding towns and cities, some because of employment concerns. Gary's fortunes have risen and fallen with those of the steel industry, and decline was brought on by growing overseas competitiveness in the steel industry that caused U.S. Steel to layoff many workers. Crime increased dramatically.

These areas were once magnificent and soon became some of the nation's most notorious ghettos. They became slums that the devil himself avoids. Because of a depraved economy, they soon became "Hell holes" and nests for drugs, gang violence and prostitution—chronic human slaughterhouses. These slums with their cheap labor are nothing more than modern day plantation slave's quarters, only in this case, the masters allow the subjects to work somewhere, purchase their own hut and buy their own food and swill. Gary, Indiana and East Orange, New Jersey, South Chicago, certain sections of Detroit, St. Louis, Memphis, Cleveland, Philadelphia, Baltimore, Los Angeles and so many other notorious ghettos in every major city across the country give perfect examples of this phenomenon.

Many of these cities are speckled with good and bad people, and it's extremely difficult for the good people to manage, while the bad ones don't really care. Furthermore, when the public schools were required to integrate by law, we gained a new meaning for the term "white lightning". The white people bolted to the suburbs so fast they created black holes in the cities that the Milky Way Galaxy would be proud of. This migration left the poor inner city school districts cash-strapped, without a healthy tax base. Along came the charter schools to devastate the public schools even more. Consider this a warning, unless we change something, keep out of Goshen!

Despite mainstream America's use of the term "ghetto" to signify a poor, culturally or racially-homogenous urban area, those living in the area often used it to signify something positive. The black ghettos did not always contain dilapidated houses and deteriorating projects, nor were all of its residents poverty-stricken. For many African Americans, the ghetto was "home": a place representing authentic blackness and a feeling, passion, or emotion derived from rising above the struggle and suffering of being black in America. Langston Hughes relays in the "Negro Ghetto" (1931) and "The Heart of Harlem" (1945): "The buildings in Harlem are brick and stone/And the streets are long and wide,/But Harlem's much more than these alone,/Harlem is what's inside."

Recently the word "ghetto" has been used in slang as an adjective rather than a noun. It is used to indicate an object's relation to the inner city or black culture, and also more broadly, and somewhat offensively, to denote something that is shabby or of low quality. While "ghetto" as an adjective can be used derogatorily, the African American community, particularly the hip hop scene, has taken the word for themselves and begun using it in a more positive sense that transcends its derogatory origins.Ghetto (from Wikipedia, the free encyclopedia)

Chapter 5

THE PRINCE'S PURVIEW

BECAUSE OF HIS PROPER EDUCATION, training and spiritual purview, Moses saw the problems plaguing his people from a higher vantage point. On an occasion, Moses witnessed an Egyptian beating a Hebrew slave. Out of his concern, Moses became an activist and promptly slew the Egyptian (Exodus 2:11-13). On the very next day, Moses happened upon two Hebrew slaves that were battling with each other. He then approaches the two and enquires of them as to why brethren strove against each other. Moses perceived that he was in deep trouble when the response to his inquiry returned the focus to him. One of the slaves replied, "Who made you the prince and judge over the Hebrew?" and,"will you kill me as you have done to the Egyptian?" Moses' involvement caused him to be evicted from the royal palace of Pharaoh and run for his life.

As I studied, I considered why the Hebrew men were at odds with each other. Could it have been that one slave had a better position than the other did? Was one moving up while the other remained stagnate? Was one a Hebrew foreman or boss? There is a phenomenon in the black community that is called the "Crab Syndrome"-as one crab climbs out of the pale another crab will grab hold of him and pull him back down, so no one escapes. As quiet as it is kept, black people don't really like other successful blacks and are jealous at times. Why is this so? Generally, but not always, successful blacks seem to have an elitist attitude that says, "If you can possibly prepare yourself as I have done, you might become successful like me one day." "Look at me; I have crossed over and I'm accepted; I'm the H.N.I.C (Head N*** =Negro in Charge)." "I'm a House N*** while you are just a Field N***." "Shoot, I'm practically white!" Never the less, Moses was the "Palace Hebrew" and for whatever reason the "Field Hebrews" didn't like him. They would "Rat" on Moses to Pharaoh to pull him down with them (blacks call this "snitchin"). In other words they were telling Moses, we don't really need your purview. Moses knew that Pharaoh would learn of the murder, so he escaped the country for his own life (Exodus 2:14-15).

In my opinion, Dr. Martin Luther King was martyred because of his purview. In his speech at the March on Washington, he stated, "America has given the Negro a bad check that has come back insufficient funds." Malcolm X was killed by so called "friendly fire", and he made this statement, "We were stripped of everything we had and cast into a fiery furnace, a land where they have made it as hot as hell for 400 years." Elijah Mohammed added this observation, "You are a part of an indoctrination that goes from generation to generation. The so called American Negro has to be completely reeducated." I will later, in this book, visit comments from the Reverend Jesse Jackson.

Through their works and lives, many princes have given their purview to a people who seemly could not really hear them, just as Moses did. Huey Newton, Medgar Evers, Eldridge Cleaver, Bobby Seal, Angela Davis, Gill Scott Heron, Samuel F. Yette, Marvin Gaye, Maya Angelou, Rosa Parks, E. Michael Dyson, Julian Bond, Marcus Garvey, Dick Gregory, Louis Farrakhan, T.D. Jakes, Oprah Winfrey, Al Sharpton and Bill Cosby have all in their own separate ways called a people to a higher conscience. Please forgive me if I didn't mention you in this stellar line-up of princes and their purviews, but there would not be enough room or time to mention you all.

The Black community hears, but Stagger Lee keeps on killing Billy. I recall the words of the movie produced by John Singleton *"Boyz in the Hood."* Ferris is addressing a group of boys in Compton, and he asks them, "Why is there a gunshop on every corner in the black community? For the same reason there's a liquor store. Why? They want us to kill ourselves; you go out to Beverly Hills you don't see that sh**." In her Lyrics, Erika Badu, points out something that people should consider: "we made a wrong turn back there somewhere." At one time the Hip-Hop community was so divided against itself that some of its super stars became immensely inflamed with each other. Some went for bad on the East Coast and some were supposedly badder on the West Coast. People took sides.

This challenge blew up way out of proportion when Tupac produced the notorious cut "Hit 'em up", culminating in the deaths of Tupac and Biggie. Believe it or not, in some places, you could be executed for wearing red or blue clothes.

Many self-styled, new ages Black achievers owe their success to the struggles of black suffrage. They thumb their noses at ideas like affirmative action and detest so-called black leaders like Jesse or Al. They feel as though the playing field is now miraculously even after all these years of oppression, and they are absolutely sure they have never received any handouts because they have worked hard for what they have accomplished. Listen, sometimes it is not what you know or what you have done, but it's who you know or who knows you that make a difference in your success. Nevertheless, they have arrived on time and are doing just fine in their own little corner of the world, until they are discovered somewhere doing something while black. Sometimes even decent or famous black people are accosted. Prominent Harvard professor and also one of the country's pre-eminent black scholars, Henry L. Gates, was arrested on July 21, 2009, for entering his own house while being black.

To all the mighty warriors, black and white, who have fought and still fight in the trenches, all is not for naught. I am grateful for the progress I see in America today. After all, America did not invent oppression and slavery, it just followed a bad pattern that had been around the world for millennia. Many black children have benefited from the civil right struggles of those that cared and dared to make a difference. Some of these children don't even realize what it took to get them where they are now. When I look at America today, I see blacks being integrated into the fabric of American society. Many black children who have stayed focused and true to their integrity have received special scholarships to college like the "Bill Gates Scholarship" and many other merit awards. Some have forged their way in junior colleges, in nursing and trade schools, realizing education is going to be the key that unlocks the doors to a better society and life for them and their families. Many are fulfilling Dr. Martin Luther King's dream of participating in a society that recognizes their skill sets and character and not just the color of their skin. Brilliant minded young blacks are gaining significance in all fields, and some have become CEOs, presidents, directors, senior partners, specialists, technicians, team leaders, medical doctors, pharmacists, attorneys—the list goes on. Special thanks to all the people who have put aside former oppressive concepts and moved forward to a new and improved society. This pleases God who has given gifts of all kinds to all of mankind.

Chapter 6

PITHOM AND RAMESES

Biblical Rameses

THE BOOK OF EXODUS MENTIONS "Rameses" as one of the cities on whose construction the Israelites were forced to labor. Understandably, this Rameses was identified by an early generation of biblical archaeolgists with the Pi-Rameses a city built by Rameses II. When the 21st Dynasty moved the capital to Tanis, Pi-Rameses was abandoned became a quarry for monuments, but it was not forgotten: its name appears in a list of 21st Dynasty cities, and it had a revival under Sheshong I (the biblical *Shishak*) of the 22nd Dynasty (10th century BC), who tried to emulate the achievements of Rameses. The existence of the city as Egypt's capital as late as the 10th century means it is thus not possible to say that the reference to Rameses in the Exodus story preserves a genuine memory of the era of Rameses II; and indeed, the shortened form "Rameses", in place of the original Pi-Rameses, is first found in 1st millennium texts.

The bible describes Rameses as a "store-city". The exact meaning of the Hebrew phrase is not certain, but it suggests a supply depot on or near the frontier. This would be an appropriate description for Pithom (*Tel al-Maskhuta*) in the 6th century BC, but not for the royal capital in the time of Rameses, when the nearest frontier was far off in the north of Syria. Only after the original royal function of Pi-Rameses had been forgotten could the ruins have been re-interpreted as a fortress on Egypt's frontier.

Biblical Pithom

Pithom is one of the cities which, according to Exodus 1:11, was built for the Pharaoh of the oppression by the forced labor of the Israelites. The other city was Rameses; and the Septuagint adds a third, "*On, which is Heliopolis.*" The meaning of the term, rendered in the Authorized Version "treasure cities" and in the Revised Version "store cities," is not definitely known.

You must build our commercial center and commerce, but there will be no record in Egypt that you did anything. In fact, as time moves forward, we can barely find a trace of your contribution in our books and histories. Just what did you do? We built this city ourselves.

Not many people know that the great cities of Pithom and Rameses in Egypt were built by Hebrew people (Exodus 1:11). Beside the biblical account, the records are fuzzy. Egypt's majesty belongs solely to the Egyptians. Pharaoh assigned taskmasters over the Hebrews and caused them to serve with rigor and make their lives bitter. They were commanded the detail of making brick, and the tale of bricks were never diminished even when the essential components of the bricks were withheld. With daily arduous labor they built the treasure cities to store all the riches of mighty Pharaoh.

It's traumatizing to realize that you weren't even mentioned in the credits for a masterpiece that you designed or played a major role in. Someone else is beaming with pride while you feel forlornly violated. Infringement takes all of the wind out of your sail, but you must forge ahead and transform or evolve. America is the mightiest country in the world today and is truly a superpower without peer. Just as Rome was not built in a day, America took many hands, backs, minds and lives for us to arrive at our present locality. America is a land of mingled people; it's born of many immigrants. It belongs to the people (*E Pluribus Unum*, out of many one), and not to one race of individuals, even though they may represent the majority of the populace. The soil of America has drunk the blood of almost every type of man. We the people built America.

American history books omit many of the key characters, mistakenly and deliberately. This placated those who were mentioned, who are proud of their accomplishments while casting the forgotten into Oblivion. If you would read some historical accounts and view some motion picture renditions, you might conclude that the American Indian was a beast or animal and that the Africans didn't possess enough gray matter to tie their shoes, if they even wore them. The truth is, Native Americans had civilization, and the black man has been responsible for many useful inventions and contributions. According to records kept by the White House Historical Association, slaves worked as carpenters and brick masons building the White House and the Capitol building (reported by Susan Roesgen and Aaron Cooper CNN 12/20-08). I hope you investigate the variety of ways African Americans helped this country become the great superpower we are proud of today, but I will not dwell on it here.

A few years ago America celebrated its two hundredth birthday, and she was peacock proud of her freedom. Since independence from Great Britain, she has eclipsed her mother and has become the dominant figure in the world. She sets the pace for and controls the majority of global activities. Everyone wants to be like her or desires to come to her, for she exemplifies the best the earth has to offer. She is a golden cup in the hand of the Lord. It is touted that God shed his grace on her, and I believe that to be so. But now she is experiencing internal demise.

I have never seen a time such as this-it's a time in which the people openly lambast their leaders. In times past you would have been killed for speaking against your king or leader; you would have probably spoken very quietly for fear that a little birdie would hear and would carry your words and expose you to the authorities. People today have no fear of the consequences for their actions, and they shoot out the lip and say whatever they desire.

The day of respect is long gone. Some people have always found reasons for disagreement with presidents and heads of state concerning laws and regulations that they proposed to implement during their tenure. People were disappointed but generally accepted it and voted more carefully for their leader the next time. Now anyone can openly defy and challenge the president. I realize, by our constitution, we have freedom of speech in America, but some of the things I hear on cable news networks today are akin to treason and sound like a blatant coup. Freedom demands the need for personal constraints or else we'll run amuck. I wonder why companies even lend their products for sponsorship of these demeaning broadcasts, but people generally put their money where their mouth is.

People detest our sitting president so harshly that they criticize everything and anything he does. When the critics finally win office again, they will almost take a Nazarite vow to cut off all the people that supported this president only to appease their own cronies. They will reverse his laws and then a faction of the American people will detest them also and begin the reciprocation process all over again. President Obama is, in my opinion, a brilliant man and not just a brilliant black man. He is doing the best he can to advance this country, provide some equity and sanity here and abroad. Moderately significant and virtually insignificant people and candidates belt out, "What has he done? He has absolutely no experience, and he just doesn't understand these complex situations as we do!" Well go on, smite your own leader or disclaim him so the world and the enemies of America can brainstorm and reflect on us and try to find a wedge some way, somewhere, some how. They are desperately looking for one. Ask Troy about that Greek horse. If you don't like the president, America, and your enemies surely don't like him, America, you both have something in common. Two enemies of each other oxymoronically agree. You both loathe the American president.

Jesus once said, "A city divide against itself **SHALL NOT STAND**." (Mathew 12:25), yet we keep going headlong toward the abyss. It appears that we will not stop all the bickering between the parties until we are a plume of smoke. Everyone is definitely a patriot on the right hand and left side of the aisle, but who genuinely cares about America? Hereafter, how shall we appear in history? We had better hope and pray that America is not the economical Babylon of the scriptures, the Babylon that meets sudden destruction in one hour

9 And the kings of the world who committed adultery with her and enjoyed her great luxury will mourn for her as they see the smoke rising from her charred remains.

10 They will stand at a distance, terrified by her great torment. They will cry out, "How terrible, how terrible for you, O Babylon, you great city! In a single moment God's judgment came on you."

11 The merchants of the earth will weep and mourn for her, because there will be no more markets for their cargo:

12 their cargo of gold, silver, precious stones, and pearls; fine linen, purple silk, and scarlet cloth; fragrant wood of every kind, all articles of ivory and all articles of the most expensive wood, bronze, iron, and marble;

13 cinnamon, spice, incense, myrrh, frankincense, wine, olive oil, fine flour, wheat, cattle, sheep, horses, carriages, slaves, and human lives.

14 The merchants will say, "Babylon, the good things you wanted have gone from you. All your rich and fancy things have disappeared. You will never have them again."

15 The merchants who became rich from selling to her will be afraid of her suffering and will stand far away. They will cry and be sad

16 and say: "Terrible! How terrible for the great city! She was dressed in fine linen, purple and red cloth, and she was shining with gold, precious jewels, and pearls!

17 All these riches have been destroyed in one hour!" Every sea captain, every passenger, the sailors, and all those who earn their living from the sea stood far away from Babylon.

18 They will cry out as they watch the smoke ascend, and they will say, "Where is there another city as great as this?"

[19] And they threw dust on their heads and cried out, weeping and being sad. They said: "Terrible! How terrible for the great city! All the people who had ships on the sea became rich because of her wealth! But she has been destroyed in one hour!"
(Excerpts from Revelations 18. NLT)

"Come on guys, let's change our textbooks to suit our own platform and give our own party the advantage; forget the facts, and let's make history become HIS STORY; our great state will resign from this union and disregard any law we disagree with; we have our own flag, Mr. Lincoln, so if they don't play the game like we like it, we will take our ball and go home." This is our folly we finagle with on a daily basis. Some say we need illegal immigrants in order to maintain our economy, while others say "Head 'em up and move 'em out!" Remember they are only here anyway because somebody is benefiting from their services and hiring them. Make up your mind America, what do you want? A double-minded man is unstable in all of his ways and will not receive anything from God. He will be tossed by every wind of doctrine coming down the pike. Pharaoh's dilemma has come to America.

Chapter 7

WHO IS GOD?

PHARAOH WAS REVERED AS GOD, in ancient Egypt. Ancient Egyptians adored a plethora of other idols, worshipping figures like Apis (bull), Osiris, Sun Ra and Horus. There appears to be driving force in mankind to privately satisfy an internal void that demands reasons for all this wonderful existence. A person's existence in this complex cellular environment has to be the responsibility of something greater. An ancient emanation explosion that created all this takes considerably more faith than believing a God created it all. Pondering and searching the realm of their imaginations, people come to mere reasonable conclusions that suggest further concepts, which formulate an acceptable form of God. God to him can be multi-faceted, or there may be many different gods. Some centuries after the Pharaoh's gods, the Apostle Paul preached to some Greek multi-god worshippers on Mar's Hill a sermon revealing the one omnipotent true God of the Hebrews (Acts 17:16-34). Pharaoh had surmised that the Hebrew's rendition of God was no different than his own gods, magicians, sorceress, devotion or beliefs. In fact, Pharaoh's magicians performed some of the same feats that Moses performed in the beginning. Pharaoh then refused to allow Moses and the Hebrew people go and worship their so-called God. After all, who was the God of the Hebrews, and why should he receive adoration understanding he is not an Egyptian God?

We have not advanced very far from those ancient concepts of God. We currently do not worship the Gods of yesteryear, which we sometimes find humorous and entertaining when they are depicted in our motion pictures and cartoons. But just as those beliefs and concepts of God were very real to them, our concepts of God and science permeate our lives. We are still superstitious and trust in luck, chance and charms. We play the lottery, go to Vegas or call a psychic and so on. Every day someone is duped because the con man knows that people are looking for their one lucky day. When someone wins, that's more reason to believe.

One time I didn't follow my normal routine at school of solving mathematical equations on the board so that the adult students could see how to arrive at the answer. After class, a young lady came to me and asked why I didn't solve the answer to a particular problem on the board? "I have been winning the lottery with the numbers in your answers." she replied. I thought to myself, "Well God, I'm good for something." On another occasion, a student handed me a note that prompted me to play a certain number on Christmas Eve. She emphatically urged me to be sure to play that number on Christmas Eve. When we returned to school after winter recess, she came to me beaming with energy and pride and asked me how happy I was. It took me a minute to realize what she was referring to. She said, "You mean to tell me that you didn't play that number I gave you!" I don't believe or trust in chance, (Deuteronomy 18:10) so I had not. She had played that number straight and boxed and won $5000. I checked to see if it had really fallen as she had said, and it was so. Above that, a colleague of mine, who had shared the same classroom with me and struggled financially, won $9 million in the super lotto game. I mentioned before about a very resourceful people.

In the Last days the Bible warns that many scoffers will appear asking, "Where is the promise of His coming? Everything continues as it has been since time began" (2 Peter 3:3-4). They convince themselves that these catastrophic events are natural. Seismologist will most definitely claim that the frequency of earthquakes is not unusual, but the data reporting and recording has greatly improved. "There is really not a need for undue alarm; there are reasonable explanations for whatever we are experiencing. We can ride these present storms out, and we will be just fine. Please don't place confidence in alarmists," they will probably tell you. I am not really an alarmist; I just believe I will trust the biblical account of what we are experiencing rather than solely trust in some scientific data (Mathew 24:7-8). Knowing the data just won't comfort you when floods engulf your property, and the West Nile Virus or pestilence consumes you. Pharaoh had that same sort of notion about things when the plagues began to occur in Egypt. The plagues grew more and more severe, destroying the premises of all Egypt's gods and ruining their economy. Pharaoh's people knew it was time to release the Hebrews (Exodus 10:7), but Pharaoh did not realize that the world was being determined from another realm. He was not familiar with the one God who rules the whole world and sets the time spans for the periods of this earth. Pharaoh did not realize that those plagues Egypt was experiencing were actually a form of contractions. Our thoughts are not as God's because God has the ultimate purview and the absolute power.

In America, there are many churches of various denominations and non-denominations. There seems to be a church on every block, and there are as many worship centers as there were idols in ancient Egypt. If God were a brand, he would over stock the shelves of a great supermarket. People choose churches like smokers request brands of cigarettes: with filters, non filters, milds, longs, menthol, menthol lites, low tar, extras, filter kings, black and mild, in the flip top box, soft pack and so on. For a non-smoker, I am astounded how smokers request and know exactly which ones they want, and they know the difference in taste and exactly how to request their brand. You need a college degree to choose a pack of squares. I'm sure non-Christians peer at Christendom in a similar puzzled fashion. Worshippers boast that they are a Baptist, a Southern Baptist, Primitive Baptist, Roman Catholic, Methodist, Presbyterian, Episcopalian, Lutheran, African Methodist Episcopalian, Overcoming Holiness, COGIC, Apostolic, Mormon, Church of Christ, Christian Science, non denominational and so on and so on. Paul said that for whatever reason people were serving he thanked God that Christ is being preached. Furthermore, worship today is basically tax exempt and very lucrative. Money drives society, so many people have made being a spiritual leader their vocation whether called of God or not.

Just as Egypt perceived Pharaoh as God, many of these worship leaders have poised themselves as lords over God's heritage. Some are even viewed as an epiphany to the people. The church at Corinth experienced this seemingly harmless form of idolatry also, but Paul had to rectify that situation quickly (I Corinthians 1: 11-15). The church at Corinth was guilty of having men's person in admiration. Some claimed that they were followers of Paul, and some said that they were of Apollos and some of Cephas. People follow today's leaders in similar fashion.

Some of today's spiritual leaders have found a clever new way to become a CEO. Some have doctorates from schools without real accreditation, and baccalaureate degrees that you can receive in almost a week's time. Men love titles. What does their title really mean to God? Is God impressed by their credential, and does God really need accreditation for his ministry when God can speak through a donkey, a rock or a rooster? I think not. He has just chosen the foolishness of preaching for mankind. Today men need titles to justify their ministry to the scrutinizing world. The scrutinizing world might not think that they are crazy or foolish if they have a title added to their name. They suddenly become somebody important. They don't want to be perceived as insane like Paul was when he expounded before King Agrippa (Acts 26:24). The truth is, some of those way-out titles confirm to the scrutinizing world that what they believe is so. If you show them the power of God as Paul did, they too will believe. I would rather see the power of God manifested than to hear a hermeneutically correct sermon.

But the sheep (laymen) are very gullible, and will surrender their whole house and pocketbook to the "wolf in sheep clothing". Two women ministerial friends of mine, who have been somewhat spiritual guides for me since my youth, told me of this episode they had experienced one time as they traveled to a far city to partake in a large spiritual conference. While at one of the sessions, during the offertory section, the leader requested that everyone in the entire room reach deep into his or her purses and remove the absolute largest bill they possessed, no matter how large the denomination, and place it in the basket for offering. Being obedient as they are, they did so exactly when they marched around. When they returned to their seats, they looked at each other simultaneously, and with a somewhat bewilderment, it dawned on them what they had done with their conference money; they said to each other, "We've been had!" These idol shepherds are nothing like the shepherd Moses. Moses was the meekest man on the planet, but they are the boldest, most condescending, and demand luxury and respect while other men have died and are dying just for the gospel. Please stop commanding specific amounts of offering from the people and contracts or pledges under pressure. Allow them to give whatever they want to give to God freely. God loves a cheerful giver and not a reluctant one.

1 Then the Lord spoke to Moses, saying:
2 "Speak to the children of Israel, that they bring Me an offering. From everyone who gives it willingly with his heart you shall take My offering.
3 And this is the offering which you shall take from them: gold, silver, and bronze;
4 blue, purple, and scarlet thread, fine linen, and goats' hair;
5 ram skins dyed red, badger skins, and acacia wood;
6 oil for the light, and spices for the anointing oil and for the sweet incense;
7 onyx stones, and stones to be set in the ephod and in the breastplate.
8 And let them make Me a sanctuary, that I may dwell among them."
(Excerpts from Exodus chapter 25 NKJV)

Someone could give precious gold while another could give plain yarn, but each gift was pleasingly acceptable to God. Nobody feels bad when they give what they can and they are happy about whatever they have given to God. Don't make me pledge gold when all I own is brass. In fact, don't make me pledge at all, but allow me the space to consider my sacrifice before God. People feel bad when they give under duress, and why should people dread their service to God? God is not penurious, and he is rich beyond our imagination and full of grace. In the second letter to the Corinthians, Paul taught diligently about the church collection.

The primary purpose of the collection at that time was to aid the poor saints in Jerusalem, and so that there could be equity amongst the people in the churches of God. It was not so that they could have a grander place of worship or because a leader wanted to be wealthy. Paul made it clear that he would not take any of that money. God does not want the filthy rich sitting on the same pew with someone desperately poor. Just because you are the leader, you are not entitled to the lion's share of the collection of God. God wants equity. God does not want you to be under a strain supporting the church while the leaders are living large and the church is prospering. God wants equity. Listen to what Paul taught the Corinthians and pattern yourself accordingly.

12 Whatever you give is acceptable if you give it eagerly. And give according to what you have, not what you don't have.
13 Of course, I don't mean your giving should make life easy for others and hard for yourselves. I only mean that there should be some equality.
14 Right now you have plenty and can help those who are in need. Later, they will have plenty and can share with you when you need it. In this way, things will be equal.
(2 Corinthians 8:12-14 NLT)

Do not place a stumbling block before the blind. You are entitled to whatever wisdom God imparts to these shepherds, and they will appear at your service for a foreclosed tidy sum. It's a business. Now don't misinterpret me, I believe the laborer is worthy of his hire, or else why would anyone do anything? I just do not believe in hustling God. Let's not be slothful before God. The man or woman of God is entitled to receive of the people when the people give freely to God. Enjoy, but don't milk, beat and sheer the sheep every time they walk in the barn because you can.

Remember that Jesus sacrificed and gave to us freely by grace, and the minister did not. The minister is merely a vessel to be used by God. He is just an oracle of God. If this kind of language offends the minister, he's being exposed, and he sees himself more highly than he ought. He might just be the hireling and not a true shepherd, so do not worry. God can and will raise up stones to preach the Gospel. He told Elijah, who thought he was the only one remaining true and justified in God's program, that there were seven thousand dedicated people of God in Israel unbeknownst to him (1 Kings 19:18).

Jesus said that you can not serve two masters at one time, so you can't serve God and mammon (money) (Mathew 6:24). Money is not evil, but the love of money is evil. So answer this question, who are you really serving if money is your primary goal in the service, and you beg for money? I mean, you had this particular service to get money for something other than deliverance of God's people. You had this service for a pastor's anniversary or pastor's birthday party or something of that sort. If you want to give them some money, just collect it and give it to them. Don't solicit popular or unique ministries to come because they are a big draw and therefore will fatten the kitty. If you want to celebrate something, just have a celebration. Service is not a three-ring circus full of clowns and jesters: service is succinct for deliverance of the people. Don't mix the minister's honors with the worship and teaching of God's word. They are not on the same plane with God, and doing this is akin to Aaron's sons, Nadab and Abihu, offering strange fire before God (Leviticus 10: 1-2). God does not share his stage with anyone, no matter how esteemed he may be. God alone is worshipped and praised.

In the early church, the ministers visited established synagogues, the Temple and Solomon's Portico, pagan shrines, open markets, fields, houses and anywhere people met for religious purposes, but today we focus every effort and every cent solely on building the great temple. People visit them now solely to see what they look like inside or who is a member there and how do they perform. These edifices are not the churches of God; they are the administrative centers of successful church businesses. In his letter to the Corinthians, Paul plainly points out that the church is the body of Christ (the believers, wherever they reside). The Church today is well dressed, coordinated and suited down with intriguing words, catchy phrases, copycat idiosyncrasies and tired idioms, but miniscule power. We could get more results from God if we would duplicate how the apostles lived instead of how Gamaliel taught. Apostles, prophets, pastors, teachers-God is tired of your religious systems, and He will now burst out onto the streets to save his people. They will not even resemble you, so you will detest them in the same manner the Sanhedrin hated the apostles for not following their established patterns, and you will finally realize that you yourselves are the true Laodiceans.

Do you think God is poor? Look at the wealthiest people on this planet and understand this—God allows them their lot. Jesus said seek me first and I will give you the desires of your heart. Grace is free, and you can do nothing to earn it. Just receive whatever God gives you freely and contentedly and God will give you more. Remember how God gave Israel, free of charge, all that land from Lebanon to Gaza and eastward to the Euphrates River, with houses and gardens that were built by the Caananites and other nations. Their mortgage was faith and obedience. Stop using scare tactics and fearmongering to keep the coffers full. If God really began your campaign, God will finish your campaign without strain. If God wants you to have something, God will give it to you. If God gives something to someone else, God doesn't want you to have it, so don't covet. God knows exactly what you should possess. Read about God's property distributions in Deuteronomy 2 in its entirety, and you will understand somewhat how God thinks. He informs Moses what possessions God will give to them and what possessions He has given to others. He has not changed since that day.

You can not have this

5 Meddle not with them; for I will not give you of their land, no, not so much as a foot breadth; because I have given mount Seir unto Esau *for* a possession.

9 And the LORD said unto me, Distress not the Moabites, neither contend with them in battle: for I will not give thee of their land *for* a possession; because I have given Ar unto the children of Lot *for* a possession.

19 And *when* thou comest nigh over against the children of Ammon, distress them not, nor meddle with them: for I will not give thee of the land of the children of Ammon *any* possession; because I have given it unto the children of Lot *for* a possession.

You can have this

24 Rise ye up, take your journey, and pass over the river Arnon: behold, **I have given into thine hand** Sihon the Amorite, king of Heshbon, and his land: **begin to possess *it***, and contend with him in battle.

(Excerpts from Deuteronomy chapter 2 KJV)

When the children of Israel were about to leave Egypt, God commanded the Egyptians to give their precious items to God's people. God supplied his people then and God will supply his people now.

God's burdens are light. Rest from trying to make the people follow parts of the law to be saved, or remain active in your assembly or to maintain your positions. O' Galatians, we live under grace, and I'm so glad that the things and judgements that applied to old Israel were not carried over to the Gentiles. Do not confuse the people or wrest the scriptures to build your personal empire. God is not blind because He lets you keep on doing what you do, and God is most certainly not confused about rightly dividing His word. God knows what applies to this generation and some of you do, too.

Whenever a false minister wrestles the scriptures to fit them to their purpose, somehow their tenets don't perfectly align with what God's word states. They will have to fabricate something. Ask your leader if every three years you should take all of your tithes and give them to the poor and widow in your city or church? If he or she replies, "That does not pertain to us or the church" (Deuteronomy 14:28). You will understand what I am saying.

28 "At the end of every third year, bring the entire tithe of that year's harvest and store it in the nearest town.

29 Give it to the Levites, who will receive no allotment of land among you, as well as to the foreigners living among you, the orphans, and the widows in your towns, so they can eat and be satisfied. Then the Lord your God will bless you in all your work."

(Deuteronomy chapter 14:28-29 NLT)

Then ask your leader, "Why does Malachi 3:7-10, which refers to apostate Israel, absolutely pertain to the church?"

7 Yet from the days of your fathers You have gone away from My ordinances And have not kept them. Return to Me, and I will return to you," Says the Lord of hosts. "But you said, 'In what way shall we return?'"

8 "Will a man rob God? Yet you have robbed Me! But you say, 'In what way have we robbed You?' In tithes and offerings.

9 You are cursed with a curse, For you have robbed Me! Even this WHOLE NATION (The whole who? . . . . NATION).

10 Bring all the tithes into the storehouse, That there may be food in My house, And try Me now in this," Says the Lord of hosts, "If I will not open for you the windows of heaven And pour out for you such blessing That there will not be room enough to receive it."

(Excerpts from Malachi chapter 3 NKJV)

This scripture does not pertain to you either unless you are the apostate nation of Israel. Practically every church affiliation in the world comes to agreement on the issue of tithes (money), but hardly a one follows this original pattern given to Moses by God:

22 "You must set aside a tithe of your crops—one-tenth of all the crops you harvest each year.
23 Bring this tithe to the designated place of worship—the place the Lord your God chooses for his name to be honored—and EAT IT there in his presence. This applies to your tithes of grain, new wine, olive oil, and the firstborn males of your flocks and herds. Doing this will teach you always to fear the Lord your God."
24 "Now when the Lord your God blesses you with a good harvest, the place of worship he chooses for his name to be honored might be too far for you to bring the tithe.
25 If so, you may sell the tithe portion of your crops and herds, put the money in a pouch, and go to the place the Lord your God has chosen.
26 When you arrive, you may use the money to BUY ANY KIND OF FOOD YOU WANT—cattle, sheep, goats, wine, or other alcoholic drink. Then feast there in the presence of the Lord your God and celebrate with your household."
(Deuteronomy 14:22-26) NLT)

I have never seen that pattern followed in the churches. It was the **only** instruction God gave Israel for tithing.

Apostle James, of the church, did not mention tithes at all in the Jerusalem council when consulting with the apostles and defining the Gentile worshippers' requirements in the church. At its inception, this is how the apostles instructed the church:

23 This is the letter they took with them: "This letter is from the apostles and elders, your brothers in Jerusalem. It is written to the Gentile believers in Antioch, Syria, and Cilicia. Greetings!"

24 "We understand that some men from here have troubled you and upset you with their teaching, but we did not send them!

25 So we decided, having come to complete agreement, to send you official representatives, along with our beloved Barnabas and Paul,

26 who have risked their lives for the name of our Lord Jesus Christ.

27 We are sending Judas and Silas to confirm what we have decided concerning your question."

28 "For it seemed good to the **Holy Spirit** and to us to lay no greater burden on you than these few requirements:

29 You must abstain from eating food offered to idols, from consuming blood or the meat of strangled animals, and from sexual immorality. If you do this, you will do well. Farewell."

(Excerpts from Acts chapter 15 NLT)

Proverbs 3:9-10 implores you to honor God with your firstfruits, and God would bless you. If you are fortunate enough to give a tithe of your substance with a cheerful heart, I'm sure that God will bless you beyond measure. If you can't give like that, give what you can by faith cheerfully and not under pressure fearfully. It doesn't mean that you are cursed and dishonoring God as old apostate Israel did. That's no truer than not being circumcised disqualifies you from the church. Men make up stuff. Jesus said that the poor widow's offering was of more value than the offering of the wealthy.

41 He sat down opposite the treasury, and watched the crowd putting money into the treasury. Many rich people put in large sums.

42 A poor widow came and put in two small copper coins, which are worth a penny.

43 Then he called his disciples and said to them, "Truly I tell you, this poor widow has put in more than all those who are contributing to the treasury.

44 For all of them have contributed out of their abundance; but she out of her poverty has put in everything she had, all she had to live on."
(Mark 12:41-44 NRSV)

Some people pay great tithes and still dishonor God with their actions. God is faithful, and believe it or not God thoroughly understands man's pernicious ways. Go find the scripture that delineates to whom and how to pay your tithe in the church age, but don't hold your breath. God saves us by his grace alone and not by our good deeds (filthy rags Isaiah 64:6). Mechizedek, the eternal priest, received a tithe of honor from Abraham, and likewise Jesus, our eternal priest, will be honored with a tithe from you if your life honors him first. If not, keep your money because you can not purchase salvation.

9 Honor the Lord with your possessions, And with the firstfruits of all your increase;
10 So your barns will be filled with plenty, And your vats will overflow with new wine
(Proverbs 3:9-10 NKJV)

A real Christian can not double or triple harvest their fields or vineyards and not leave a gleanings for the poor in their land. You are pretty opulent, but every time someone says we should skim a little tax from the wealthiest Americans, you cry out that this is the sin of wealth transferring. You may be rich or at least greatly blessed, but if they take an extra dime of your money through taxes you will call it socialism and demand that the poor amass their own wealth. Don't give the indigent universal healthcare because it will cost our kids and us money. In fact, don't give them anything. Kill them through the methods of poverty and oppression while they are teens or adults, but please don't abort them as a fetus because God is watching us, and thou shall not kill. You get up every week and make a straight line to your church service to present yourself before some entity. It must be Chemosh, Ashteroth, Baal, Horus or Dagon, but it is not before the Lord of your Bible. You may honor God with your mouth, but your heart is elsewhere. You think that God detests the poor and loves you, but you are greatly mistaken (Deuteronomy 24:19-22). If you claim to be Christian, this is for your ears.

The Hebrews required a sign (I Corinthians 1:22-24). They really didn't believe God was speaking through Moses until he performed some miracles before their eyes. So God gave them sign after sign and also a guiding light to follow. In the Gospel age, the Pharisees, too, always requested signs from Jesus. The Greeks (Gentiles), on the other hand, required knowledge; their primary focus was on intellect. People with these two types of deliverance systems were in Egypt during the time of Moses, and people of these two types are alive and well today. A third type of individual believes in the sovereignty of God alone, without a sign or his own personal intellect, but this individual lives by simple faith. They can receive abundantly from God because God operates through faith only.

Some men feel that God is unfair because He does not fit their pattern of goodness and equity. To them, God is good to some and forsakes others. God may have unfairly taken the life of somebody they knew who was good, while sparing someone who, in their mind, should have been annihilated. God knows that good people will die and some would be killed accidentally, so God instituted cities of refuge in ancient Israel (Deuteronomy 19:4-11). But God is not right to them because they are self-righteous. Someone is thinking that God doesn't perform miracles in their sight or in their life as He did in the Bible, so his word is suspect and is not trustworthy.

Another person thinks he is smarter or wiser than God is because he is well educated and God's teachings seem barbaric or trite, and God's demands are far-fetched and hard to assimilate. He hears the Word and reads the Bible like a man that hears and reads the account of a modern day news reporter and he says, "God killed all those Egyptians yesterday because their president wouldn't allow his hostages to go free to the Sinai Desert and worship him." Then he contorts just as Pharaoh did, "Who is this God who kills people, and what kind of a crazy God would do that anyway? I know I wouldn't, so why does everybody have to go somewhere and worship him or die?" Everything must be reasonable or rational or he discredits God.

The third person simply believes God, and God simply orders his steps and teaches him the wisdom of God's creation and its pending demise. God then also promises to preserve him from the destruction of mankind. This is not the perfect person, but he keeps doing his best to follow and believe God with a true heart, and he repents and turns from his own ways. He is and will be rewarded.

How could God destroy Pharaoh's army and be without some kind of fault? Keep this in your mind and never forget it! The wicked shall be turned in to hell and all nations that forget God (Psalms 9:17). When you dismiss God from your mind and you chump him off, after a grace period, he will likewise dismiss you and chump you off also. At this point you will then be reduced in your nature to "deer meat" or "road kill"; you will, so to speak, become as a mere natural animal that was created by God for the sole purpose of being hunted, sacrificed or destroyed as prey. You become as fodder in the ecosystem, like a disgusting roach. Your soul becomes irredeemable. Ask Nebuchadnezzar (Daniel 4:25) about this process. He was turned into a bovine animal-minded person for a seven-year period, but also remember that God had mercy on him and restored his mind. In so many words, you could be considered cattle or a creeping thing roaming to and from on God's planet earth (Romans 1: 18-32). You were created to be a man, but God can turn you into anything he desires, and you could not do anything about it (Isaiah 64:8). Stubborn Jonah became whale food and lived to tell (Jonah 1:17).

If we can imagine things and create unbelievable characters in our movies and animations, God can actually do what we imagine, but I pray daily that he does not. Who could stand if he did? How would you like to see a beast from Revelations walk into your room as you watch television, and you are in your right mind? Take a visit to a slaughterhouse and consider this—beautiful animals die every day just for food, and this is acceptable to God (Deuteronomy 18:3). God is not a toy; He created it all, and you or no one will mock God or God's word. You will receive the just recompense for your choices unless you repent. Deuteronomy 7:10 says: and He repays those who hate Him to their face, to destroy them. He will not be slack with him who hates Him; He will repay him to his face.

28 And since they did not see fit to acknowledge God, God gave them up to a debased mind and to things that should not be done.
29 They were filled with every kind of wickedness, evil, covetousness, and malice. Full of envy, murder, strife, deceit, craftiness, they are gossips,
30 slanderers, God-haters, insolent, haughty, boastful, inventors of evil, rebellious toward parents,
31 foolish, faithless, heartless, ruthless.
32 They know God's decree, that those who practice such things deserve to die—yet they not only do them but also even applaud others who practice them.
(Romans 1:28-32 NRSV)

Do not imagine that destruction is what God wants for you or created you for; it's not. He really loves you immensely, but you have been given your own personal will, and you can do whatever you want to do with it because it's yours. You can choose God or not choose God like you can choose water, coffee, juice, wine, hard drink, beer or soda whichever you desire; it's your business. All of your choices may not be wise ones though. After an undetermined amount of time and you have by your will continually dissed and spurned God, He then closes the books on your chance at eternal life. That's God's business. He will answer to no one. The opinions and case arguments of those of whom you depend and trust won't amount to a hill of beans before God. In fact, the same processes and grace will be offered unto them, and they might just change their minds toward God while leaving you lost. People do change and God gives them space to do so. On an episode of Leave it to Beaver, one of Beaver's friends made a pact with him that they both would make a stupid face at the moment the photographer snapped the class picture. At first, Beaver didn't agree with the idea, but after being coaxed by his friend he agreed. At the very moment the picture was taken, Beaver's friend decided to renege and take a normal picture while leaving Beaver alone and looking stupid on the class picture. Of course, Beaver got in a lot of trouble for messing up the class picture, and his so-called friend abandoned him. Don't let this be the case with you and your agent or commandant.

That all being said and done, I will now close this book as I revisit the sayings I mentioned before from the Reverend Jesse Jackson in the chapter on the prince's purview. He was speaking to an audience at Operation Push. He was referring to the plight of the African American people, and he was very encouraging and poignant in his delivery. I will use his words to address a similar spiritual concern. He said, "We are ready for change, and whether a doctor is there or not, the water has broken, the blood is spilled, a new black member is going to be born. Cut us in or cut it out. It's a new ball game." Almost everyone is familiar with the birth of a baby and the period the follows the end of gestation. The water break is a sure sign that the unborn child is opening the womb and forging through the birth canal. The baby is finished its internal incubation period and is ready to enter this life. The contractions get closer and closer together, and the mother's pain seems unbearable. It almost and maybe at some point will make a Christian woman cuss. After all the contractions (the 10 plagues of Egypt) were settled and the cussing period was over, Pharaoh finally released the Hebrew people and thrust them out of Egypt. The Hebrew's 430-year gestation period in Egypt was complete, and the water finally broke at the Red Sea where Pharaoh's army drowned. The nation crossed through the sea's threshold (the birth canal) onto dry ground, and the new born baby Hebrew nation called Israel was delivered on the Sinai Peninsula.

From Suffering to Glory

[18] For I consider that the sufferings of this present time are not worthy *to be compared* with the glory which shall be revealed in us.

[19] For the earnest expectation of the creation eagerly waits for the revealing of the sons of God.

[20] For the creation was subjected to futility, not willingly, but because of Him who subjected *it* in hope;

[21] because the creation itself also will be delivered from the bondage of corruption into the glorious liberty of the children of God.

[22] **For we know that the whole creation groans and labors with birth pangs together until now.**

(Romans 8:18-22 NKJV)

When earthquakes, tsunamis, hurricanes, flooding cities, oil spills, terrorism, perplexities in the cities and major unrest begin to continually prevail, you are witnessing contractions of another nature. Today those ferocious contractions are getting closer and closer together. Men's hearts will fail them for fear of what's coming on the earth. Just as in Egypt, God has induced these contractions, and they are foolproof signs to mankind that something new must soon be birthed here on earth. This world is almost completely dilated, the waters are breaking, and the planet is upheaving with convulsions tremendously. Pharaoh's dilemma is appearing before our eyes. A New Kingdom is about to be birthed. This New Kingdom will be the arrival of the "Stone" that was hewn out of the mountain (Daniel 2: 34-44). This Stone is the one that was untouched by human hands. It broke down all the kingdoms of the world, and the Stone became a great mountain that filled the earth. The New Kingdom that will be birthed here will last forever (Daniel 2:44). The new king on earth is going to be **JESUS. HE IS GOD and will soon reveal himself as such**. Betters, bet on this for it will surely come to pass, but please don't procrastinate and drown or get "lullabied" in the growing tides of the ensuing red sea of bloody death and sorrows. Seek Jesus while you can.

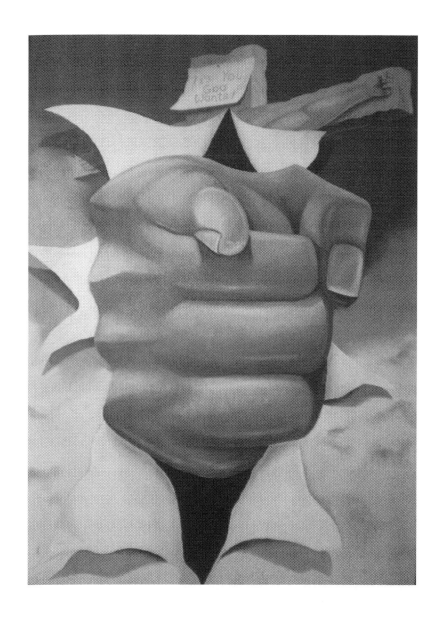

About the Artwork

All artwork by Stuart E. Heflin Sr.

The book cover	Isolation-Gestation	oils and acrylics on canvas
Picture 1	Map	Print Shop Pro
Picture 2	A Nightmare Reality	oils on canvas
Picture 3	Drown in my Tears	oils on canvas
Picture 4	Pot of Gold (Land of Nod)	oils on canvas
Picture 5	Woulda Coulda Shoulda 2	mixed sculpture photography and Photoshop
Picture 6	The Apocalypse	mixed media and oil on canvas
Picture 7	God Wants You	oil on canvas